TERRIBLE TSUNAMIS

Gareth Stevens
PUBLISHING

CHARLOTTE TAYLOR

Please visit our website, www.garethstevens.com. For a free color catalog of all our high-quality books, call toll free 1-800-542-2595 or fax 1-877-542-2596.

Cataloging-in-Publication Data
Names: Taylor, Charlotte, 1978-.
Title: Terrible tsunamis / Charlotte Taylor.
Description: New York : Gareth Stevens Publishing, 2023. | Series: Nature's revenge | Includes glossary and index.
Identifiers: ISBN 9781538280553 (pbk.) | ISBN 9781538280577 (library bound) | ISBN 9781538280560 (6pack) | ISBN 9781538280584 (ebook)
Subjects: LCSH: Tsunamis–Juvenile literature. | Natural disasters–Juvenile literature.
Classification: LCC GC221.5 T39 2023 | DDC 363.34'94–dc23

Portions of this work were originally authored by Caitie McAneney and published as *Slammed by Tsunamis*. All new material in this edition was authored by Charlotte Taylor.

Published in 2023 by
Gareth Stevens Publishing
29 East 21st Street
New York, NY 10010

Designer: Leslie Taylor
Editor: Megan Quick

Photo credits: Cover (tsunami wave) Mimadeo/Shutterstock.com; pp. 1–32 (icons-series artwork) Vector by/Shutterstock.com; pp. 1–32 (hazard tape-series artwork) DDevecee/Shutterstock.com; p. 4 Youkonton/Shutterstock.com; p. 5 (beach) Jeremy Horner/Alamy.com; p. 7 Designua/Shutterstock.com; p. 9 https://commons.wikimedia.org/wiki/File:MSH80_st_helens_eruption_plume_07-22-80.jpg; p. 11 Rainer Lesniewski/Shutterstock.com; p. 13 Kyodo/APImages.com; p. 15 capture63/Shutterstock.com; p. 17 Associated Press/APImages.com; p. 19 https://commons.wikimedia.org/wiki/File:US Navy 050119-N-2560Y-298 Aerial view of Banda Aceh, Sumatra, three weeks after a Tsunami devastated the coastal region.jpg; p. 21 Associated Press/APImages.com; p. 23 Duncan Selby/Alamy.com; p. 25 Associated Press/APImages.com; p. 27 tete_escape/Shutterstock.com; p. 29 Fajrul Islam/Shutterstock.com.

Printed in the United States of America

Some of the images in this book illustrate individuals who are models. The depictions do not imply actual situations or events.

CPSIA compliance information: Batch #CSGS23: For further information contact Gareth Stevens, New York, New York at 1-800-542-2595.

Find us on

CONTENTS

Words in the glossary appear in **bold** type the first time they are used in the text.

KILLER WAVES

The people on the beaches of Thailand had no reason to be afraid in the minutes before the world's deadliest tsunami struck. It was a warm morning and the skies were clear. Suddenly, the water pulled back into the ocean. Some curious people walked toward the water to see what was happening. Then the tsunami hit. Soon, thousands of people were missing or dead.

A tsunami may look like a wall of water, but it is actually a series of large waves. A tsunami can reach as high as a 10-story building. It may last for hours or even days. Often, people have little or no warning that a tsunami is on the way. This can lead to **disaster**.

A truck is wrapped around a tree (at left) from the tsunami that hit Thailand in 2004. Here, you can see **debris** on the beach moments after it hit. It was the deadliest ever, killing more than 220,000 people.

Wave Basics

If you've ever been to the beach, you know that the ocean is always moving. Waves crash along the coast, sometimes big and sometimes small. The waves that you see on a summer day are caused by wind blowing along the top of the water. Water contains energy, and the wind feeds that energy to create waves.

A TSUNAMI FORMS

A tsunami starts with a **disturbance** along the ocean floor. The disturbance that **triggers** the tsunami can be caused by several different events. Earthquakes, **volcanoes**, **landslides**, or even weather can start a tsunami. An earthquake is by far the most common cause.

The outer layer of Earth is made up of large masses of rock called tectonic plates. The plates, which float on a layer of hot rock, are always moving and bumping into one another. Usually one piece ends up sliding past the other. But sometimes the uneven edges of tectonic plates get stuck. As they try to keep moving, pressure builds up. When this pressure is released, an earthquake occurs.

Nature Unleashed

When a large tsunami hits an area where people live, it is called a natural disaster. A natural disaster is an event in nature that causes lots of damage. These severe events can destroy buildings, knock out power, and hurt or kill people and animals. Tsunamis are just one kind of natural disaster. Others include floods, **hurricanes**, and blizzards.

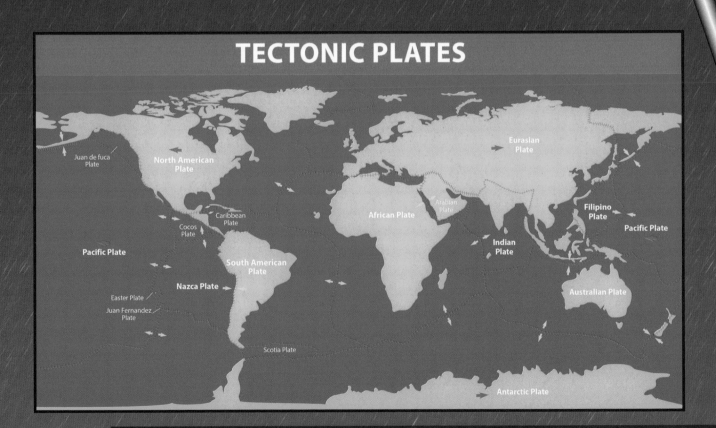

TECTONIC PLATES

Juan de fuca Plate

North American Plate

Eurasian Plate

Caribbean Plate

Arabian Plate

Cocos Plate

African Plate

Filipino Plate

Pacific Plate

Pacific Plate

Indian Plate

South American Plate

Nazca Plate

Australian Plate

Easter Plate

Juan Fernandez Plate

Scotia Plate

Antarctic Plate

The red lines on this world map show the locations of each tectonic plate. Tectonic activity causes earthquakes and tsunamis.

When a large underwater earthquake happens, the ocean floor may rise or fall. This sudden movement sends water moving in waves. The waves may build and start to travel across the ocean toward the nearest coastline.

Although it's less common, volcanoes and landslides can cause tsunamis as well. The huge force of a volcano erupting, whether it is above ground or underwater, can disturb the water and cause tsunami waves. Landslides can also cause disturbances when they send huge amounts of rock and dirt flying into the water. Landslides may happen underwater, often triggered by an earthquake. Earthquakes, volcanoes, and landslides can all set tsunami waves in motion.

Mount St. Helens Tsunami

Tsunamis do not just happen in oceans—they can strike other large bodies of water as well. On May 18, 1980, Mount Saint Helens erupted in Washington State. It was one of the biggest explosions ever in North America. The eruption caused part of the volcano to fall into Spirit Lake, which led to a tsunami 780 feet (238 m) tall.

Mount Saint Helens erupted in 1980, causing landslides, mudflows, and a tsunami.

TRACKING DOWN TSUNAMIS

The edges of tectonic plates that push against each other are called plate boundaries. Most earthquakes and tsunamis occur along plate boundaries. This is especially true in the Ring of Fire in the Pacific Ocean. This area features a string of volcanoes that developed due to tectonic plate movement. Nearly 90 percent of all earthquakes happen here. Therefore, this is the area most affected by tsunamis.

The Ring of Fire is shaped like an upside-down "U." It stretches from the southern tip of South America up to the west coast of North America to the Bering Strait and down past Japan and New Zealand. People living near the Ring of Fire are always on **alert** for earthquakes, volcanic eruptions, and tsunamis.

This map shows the Ring of Fire where tsunamis and earthquakes are most common as well as the large volcanoes found there.

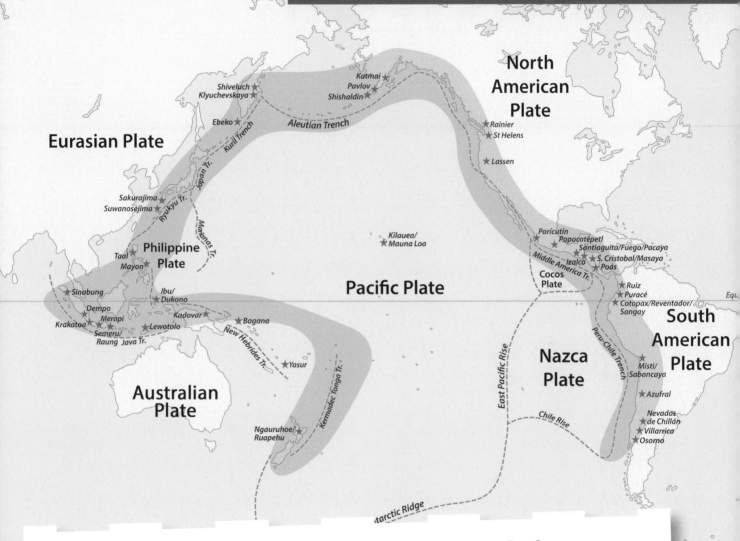

North American Plate

Eurasian Plate

Shiveluch
Klyuchevskaya
Ebeko
Aleutian Trench
Kuril Trench
Japan Tr.
Ryukyu Tr.
Katmai
Pavlov
Shishaldin
Rainier
St Helens
Lassen

Sakurajima
Suwanosejima

Marianas Tr.

Philippine Plate
Taal
Mayon

Kilauea/
Mauna Loa

Paricutin
Popocatépetl
Santiaguito/Fuego/Pacaya
Middle America Tr.
Izalco
S. Cristobal/Masaya
Poás

Cocos Plate

Sinabung
Ibu/
Dukono
Dempo
Merapi
Krakatoa
Semeru/
Raung Java Tr.
Kadovar
Bagana
Lewotolo
New Hebrides Tr.
Yasur

Pacific Plate

Ruiz
Puracé
Cotopax/Reventador/
Sangay

Equ

South American Plate

Australian Plate

Kermadec Tonga Tr.

Ngauruhoe/
Ruapehu

East Pacific Rise

Nazca Plate

Chile Rise

Peru-Chile Trench

Misti/
Sabancaya

Azufral

Nevados
de Chillán
Villarrica
Osorno

Antarctic Ridge

80

Volcanoes and the Ring of Fire

The Ring of Fire is made up of about 452 volcanoes, which is 75 percent of the world's active volcanoes. This area of the Pacific Ocean includes the Pacific Plate, a huge tectonic plate, and many smaller plates. As one plate pushes down on another, some rock melts and becomes **magma**. The magma builds up until it erupts.

ON THE MOVE

A tsunami might not look like a deadly wave at first. In fact, you might not even notice it if you were on a boat in the ocean. The water only rises about 3 feet (0.9 m) higher than usual. The ocean is so deep that this rise does not stand out.

A tsunami in the open ocean might not look scary, but it's fast. Tsunamis can travel 500 miles (804.7 km) per hour. Then, as the ocean's depth decreases, the waves start to slow down and build to greater heights. The top of each wave moves faster than the bottom, which makes them grow taller. Some waves may reach 100 feet (30.5 m), but most are less than 10 feet (3 m) tall.

Powerful tsunami waves slammed into the Japanese city of Natori in 2011.

A Long Way to Travel

With their great speed, tsunamis can cover lots of ground in a short time. Some tsunami waves travel thousands of miles to a coastline without losing energy. They can even cross an entire ocean in one day. One giant tsunami began near Chile and reached Japan in less than 24 hours.

PATH OF DESTRUCTION

In the moments before a tsunami arrives, the ocean may pull back, exposing the ocean floor. Then, the first wave slams into shore and the destruction begins. Ships and fishing boats may be pushed miles inland. People and animals on shore can be swept up and thrown down. They may be pulled into the ocean. Buildings along the coastline are smashed. Telephone lines, power lines, and bridges may be knocked down. Cars and trees may be picked up and carried away by the water.

Major flooding may reach miles away from shore. In a powerful tsunami, the first wave alone may destroy everything in its path. Remember, a tsunami is a series of waves, so they may continue to slam the shore for many hours.

In 2018, a tsunami and earthquake wrecked this neighborhood in Indonesia.

Local Tsunamis

Tsunamis can travel thousands of miles before they hit land. But some tsunamis don't have far to go. They are known as local tsunamis, and they begin less than 62 miles (100 km) or one hour before they hit the coast. Local tsunamis are very dangerous because people have little or no warning that they are coming.

AFTER THE TSUNAMI

A tsunami can last for hours or even days. But once it is over, the destruction remains. Some people may have lost their lives. Others may have lost their homes as well as basic supplies like food and clean drinking water. The entire **infrastructure** of a town or city may be destroyed.

Tsunamis cause massive flooding, which can interfere with sewage and drinking water systems. Floodwater that's full of sewage can spread disease. Diseases such as malaria are spread by mosquitoes, which live near standing water. People may die because of a lack of clean water to drink and use.

The strongest tsunami ever recorded in Japan crashed onto its northeast coast in 2011.

Japan's Great Loss

One of the most destructive tsunamis ever occurred on the coast of Japan on March 11, 2011. A huge earthquake caused a tsunami that slammed into the city of Sendai. One wave rushed 6 miles (9.7 km) inland. The tsunami hit a **nuclear** power plant in Fukushima and led to dangerous explosions. In all, more than 18,000 people died.

INDIAN OCEAN DISASTER

The deadliest tsunami in modern history began in the Indian Ocean. On December 26, 2004, a strong earthquake near the island of Sumatra caused huge waves to move out in all directions. Those waves were part of a tsunami that crashed into a dozen countries, including Malaysia, Indonesia, Thailand, the Maldives, and Madagascar. The tsunami even reached Africa—nearly 3,000 miles (4,828 km) away.

Along the coast, people on the beaches were swept away when the first waves hit. Many were unable to escape to higher ground. Many of those who died were children who weren't strong enough to hold on to anything. Within a few hours, tens of thousands were dead or missing.

Survivor Stories

People who lived through the tsunami of 2004 have shared horrifying stories of being swept into dark water by strong, fast waves. As they were tossed around, they were slammed into walls and hit with **debris** in the water. Many managed to survive by hanging onto trees or climbing onto rooftops.

A view from above shows the destruction of Banda Aceh in Indonesia, the first big city to be slammed by powerful tsunami waves in 2004.

19

HELPING HANDS

Once a tsunami hits, many people jump in to help. Search-and-rescue teams go to the site of a tsunami as soon as the waves stop completely. They search through the wreckage for survivors. Emergency workers may use dogs to help find people who are trapped under debris or in damaged buildings. Others may be floating in the open ocean, waiting to be rescued.

Some people may survive but they are seriously hurt. They need to be rushed to a hospital or have their wounds treated at the site. Aid organizations send fresh food, water, and other supplies to areas that have been hit by tsunamis.

A Long Road

Helping the victims of a tsunami goes well beyond the days and weeks right after the event. Recovery may take years. Buildings, homes, schools, and businesses need to be rebuilt. Transportation, communication, and systems like water and electricity, may also need to be restored. There are groups around the world who help people recover after disasters.

Firefighters search for victims after a tsunami hit the coast of Chile in 2010.

SOUNDING THE ALARM

Many people have been killed or hurt by tsunamis because they did not have time to move somewhere safe. Predicting when and where a tsunami might happen can save lives by giving people a chance to escape. Even a few minutes can mean the difference between life and death.

The Pacific Tsunami Warning Center (PTWC) in Hawaii is an important tsunami watch group. Experts there look at seismic, or earthquake, activity. They also study the ocean's conditions. If it seems that a tsunami is possible, the PTWC warns all areas that may be in danger. Some at-risk places alert people through text messages and other warning systems. Tsunami sirens, or alarms, may go off to warn people to get to a safe place.

TSUNAMI INFORMATION
WHEN AN OFFICIAL TSUNAMI WARNING IS ISSUED, THE SIREN WILL GIVE A LOUD WAILING TONE.

THE WEDGE

This map is intended to show the Tsunami Hazard Zone for evacuation purposes near the Wedge. The Tsunami Hazard Zone is identified using the best available data. In the event of an earthquake or an official tsunami warning, move inland and to higher ground to an area beyond the Tsunami Hazard Zone.

LEGEND

- Evacuation Zone
- Evacuation Route
- Siren Location

The City of Newport Beach makes no warranties regarding the accuracy of this map or the data from which the map was derived.

OFFICIAL TSUNAMI WARNING PROCEDURES

TSUNAMI HAZARD ZONE
IN CASE OF EARTHQUAKE GO TO HIGH GROUND OR INLAND

1. Move to high
2. Seek further
3. Follow direct

MONTHLY TEST

The City tests its Outdoor Emergency Notification System on the first Friday of every month at 12 p.m. for a brief period of time at a reduced sound level. When activated for actual emergency notifications, the sirens will sound for an extended time at a much higher sound level.

A sign in Newport Beach, California, explains what to do when sirens sound, a part of the state's early warning system for tsunamis.

New and Improved Technology

Japan had an early warning system in place when a huge earthquake and tsunami hit in 2011, and it saved lives. The country now has new technology, so if something like that happens again, they will know even sooner when an earthquake or tsunami is coming. Every second counts when preparing for a natural disaster.

SUNDA STRAIT

On December 22, 2018, a tsunami formed in the Sunda Strait, a body of water in Indonesia between the islands of Java and Sumatra. Seismic activity is common in the area, and tsunami warning systems were in place. But no warnings were ever given. More than 420 people were killed on the two islands.

Scientists believe that the tsunami occurred when the nearby Anak Krakatau volcano exploded and then partly collapsed. The collapse caused an underwater landslide, which then caused the tsunami. The early warning system only worked to detect and warn about earthquakes, not volcanoes. No one knew it was coming, so hundreds lost their lives.

Anak Krakatau erupted in July 2018, several months before a larger explosion triggered a deadly tsunami.

Krakatau's Parent

The 2018 eruption in the Sunda Strait was not the first disaster in that spot. In 1883, a volcano called Krakatau erupted, causing huge tsunami waves and killing about 36,000 people. Most of Krakatau was destroyed in the eruption, but over time, the volcano started to regrow. It was named Anak Krakatau, which means "child of Krakatau."

BE SMART, ACT FAST

Tsunami warning systems have become more exact and widely used. If you receive a tsunami warning, get to higher ground. Beaches and low-lying areas aren't safe. Tsunamis can rush miles inland, so even if you can't see the ocean, you should still listen to the warning. A good place to go is up a large hill, away from the beach.

Some people become stuck inside buildings. However, if a tall building is made of sturdy material, such as concrete, go to the highest point to find safety. Most small buildings, such as houses, aren't safe. Many places have **evacuation** sites for people to go to in case of an emergency.

Plan Ahead

It's a good idea to have a plan in place well before a tsunami warning is issued. If you live in or visit a high-risk area, make sure you know how to receive warnings (you can usually sign up for text messages). Have an emergency plan for evacuation and family communication. Know where to go and practice walking the route.

Many places at risk for tsunamis will have signs like this one pointing to escape routes.

A CLIMATE CHANGE CONNECTION?

Around the world, the climate is changing. Our planet is getting warmer, glaciers are melting, and sea levels are rising. Some scientists say that these higher water levels will lead to more destructive tsunamis as flooding moves inland. Climate change may also lead to more rainfall, which in turn causes landslides that can trigger tsunamis.

People can take steps to slow down climate change. But they cannot prevent disasters like tsunamis from happening. Like storms and earthquakes, they are a natural but dangerous part of life on Earth. We can try to learn from these events so we are better prepared for the next big one.

Curbing Climate Change

Human activities like driving cars and heating or cooling our homes are partly to blame for global warming. These activities send gases into the atmosphere where they are trapped and heat up Earth. You can help slow down global warming by doing small things like turning off lights when you leave a room or shutting off your computer when you're not using it.

A family looks around at the **destruction** left by the 2018 tsunami in Indonesia.

GLOSSARY

alert: the state of being ready for something you have been warned about

debris: the remains of something that has been broken

destruction: the state of being destroyed or ruined

disaster: an event that causes much suffering or loss

disturbance: a change in the position of something

evacuation: the act of leaving an area because of danger

hurricane: a powerful storm that forms over water and causes heavy rainfall and high winds

infrastructure: the basic structures and systems that an area needs to function properly

landslide: the sudden movement of rocks and dirt down a hill or mountain

magma: hot, liquid rock inside Earth

nuclear: having to do with the power created by splitting atoms, the smallest bits of matter

trigger: to cause

volcano: an opening in a planet's surface through which hot, liquid rock sometimes flows

FOR MORE INFORMATION

BOOKS

Farndon, John. *Extreme Earthquakes and Tsunamis*. Minneapolis, MN: Lerner, 2018.

Jackson, Tom. *How Do We Stop Climate Change?* New York, NY: Earth Aware Editions Kids, 2021.

Jenkins, Steve. *Disasters by the Numbers*. New York, NY: Clarion Books, 2021.

WEBSITES

NASA Climate Kids: Weather and Climate
climatekids.nasa.gov/menu/weather-and-climate/
Check out articles, videos, and photos about our changing planet.

NASA Space Place: What Is a Tsunami?
spaceplace.nasa.gov/tsunami/en/
Find out more about how tsunamis form and what tools are used to track them.

Weather Wiz Kids: Tsunami
weatherwizkids.com/?page_id=100
Learn more cool facts and watch a video of real tsunami waves.

INDEX